Ripples

a journey through belonging

creative life story memories

10 poems with photos
and personal endnotes

Kay Underdown

Ripples
a journey through belonging
creative life story memories
10 poems with photos
and personal endnotes

Kay Underdown

Published Summer 2023
Waves and Pebbles Publishing

I am a leaf of life

Time

Time . . .
Find it where you will
find it where you can
it never seems to be there
so find where it began
Time . . .
Where did it come from
and where did it go
how can I find it
and how will I know
Time . . .

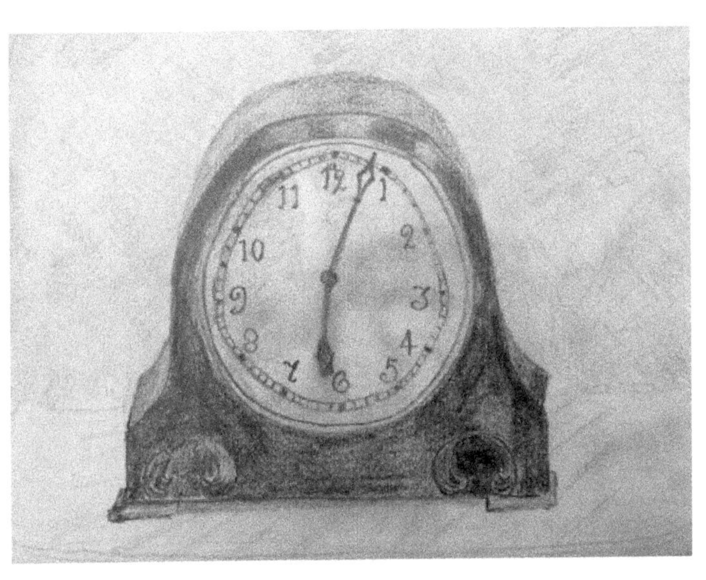

Windmill wandering
meandering green-land downs
home where I belong

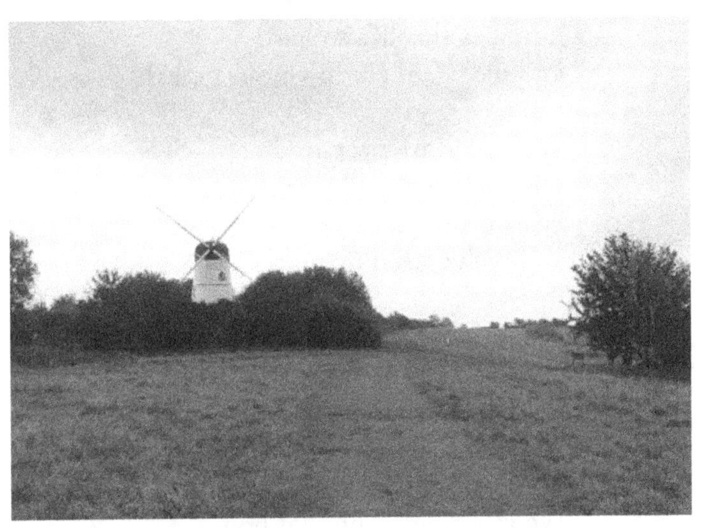

Paradice

There's nowhere I can go
you spread your blanket high
I'm trapped within this box
and I don't have any socks

How can it really be
you flutter from the sky
it makes this life so hard
and we've taken down our guard

We never are prepared
you make us really sigh
it brings us to a halt
and we've used up all the salt

Then suddenly it comes
to those that do not cry
it takes away the stress
and don't even have to dress

We're stranded here at home
with no-one coming by
it brings such wondrous calm
and don't come to any harm

There's some that have a go
don't stop to think of why
it may be hard to see
and they may just hit a tree

We ventured for a walk
you felt so very dry
the world it did stand still
and with magic we did chill

Laughter rippled through us
a warm tear filled the eye
with luck did surely dice
and we fell for paradice

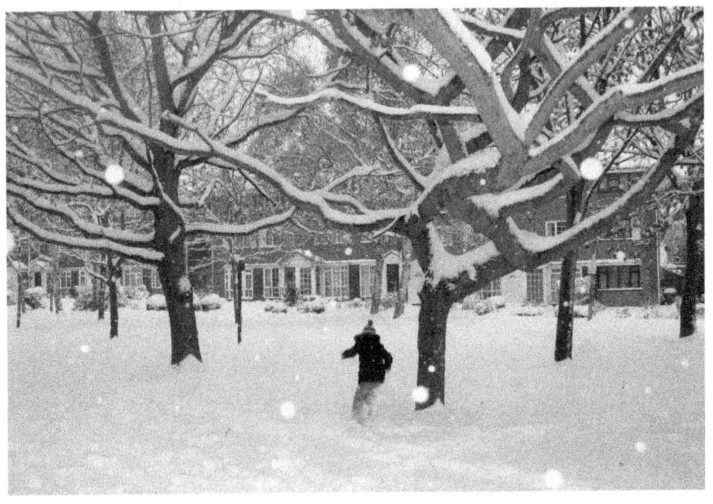

Furry Magical Moments

Tinkering silence
captures furry fingers, framing food

Time wafts
as nature disperses
magical moments, meandering mood

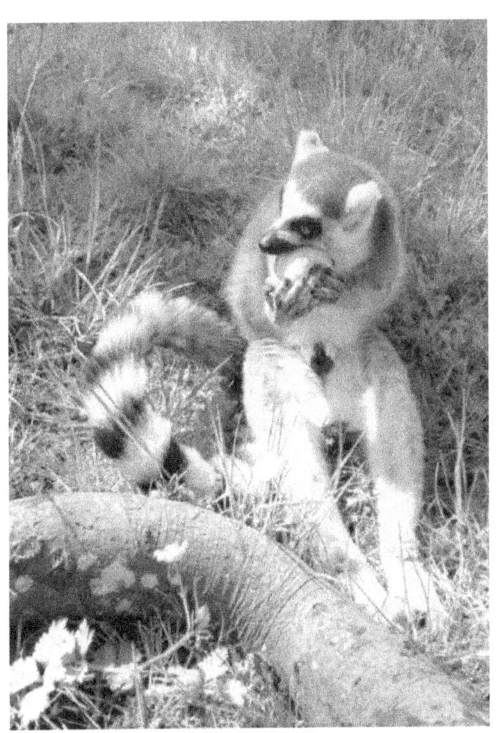

After Tenby

Happiness draws me through the tunnel of light

the whispers so precious have given me fight

Where will it take me? ☆Oh I know not for sure

but now it's life's journey, so precious, so pure

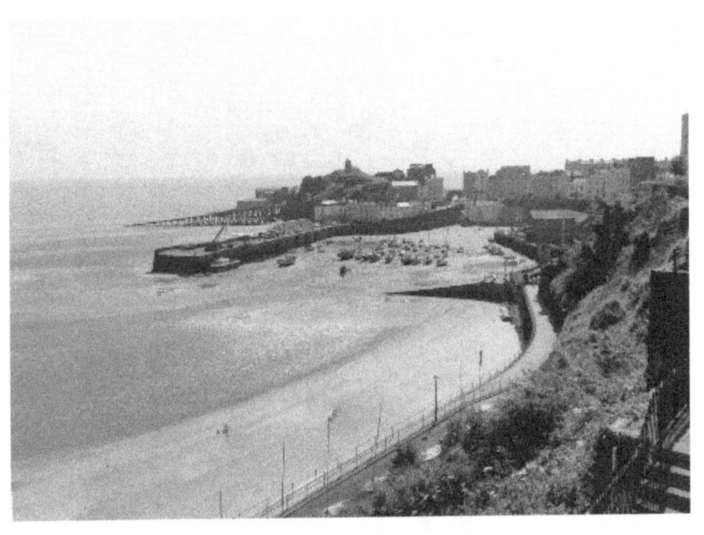

I am Life

I am a leaf
growing out a place
I live here
here on the bank

The trains pass me by
no one sees
'cept those frustrated
with their time-thieved lives
and they are too blinkered
to see

I am a leaf of life

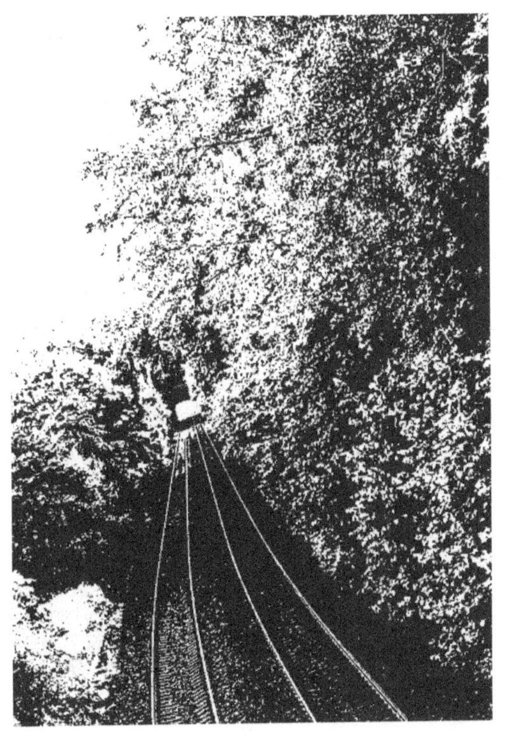

Clouds

Wishing I was up amongst the clouds
gliding serenely o'er the world
Stretched out on the emerald pillow
the sapphire canvas blotched with stately mounds
Zooming beyond the realms of living land
the magical marshmallow mountains
bestow a safe haven in my mind

Clouds are forever there, part of living
bumbling along, swept by the whipping winds of fury
Today their blackened stains threaten
till the wands of wetness streak down
A passing theme in our lives
a cloudless sky perfection seems
yet without clouds life would pass us by

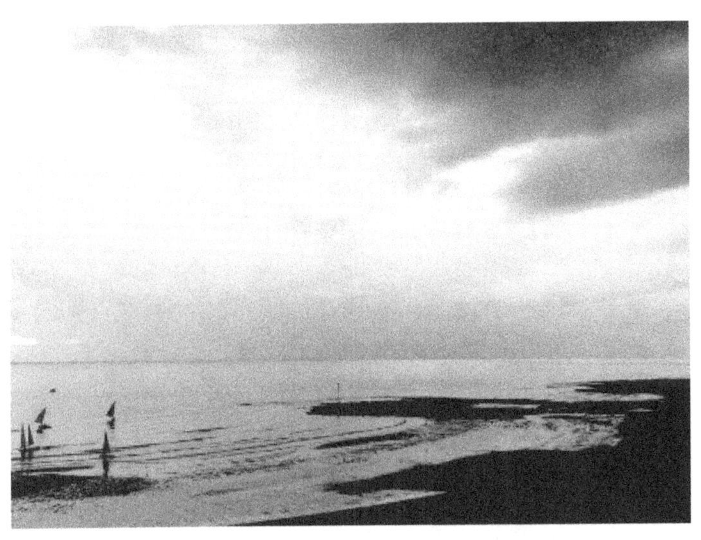

Seaside Community

The sea of friendship
is yours to discover
on your journey in life

Our memories of the ocean
will linger on
long after our footprints
in the sand are gone

The sea speaks of friendship

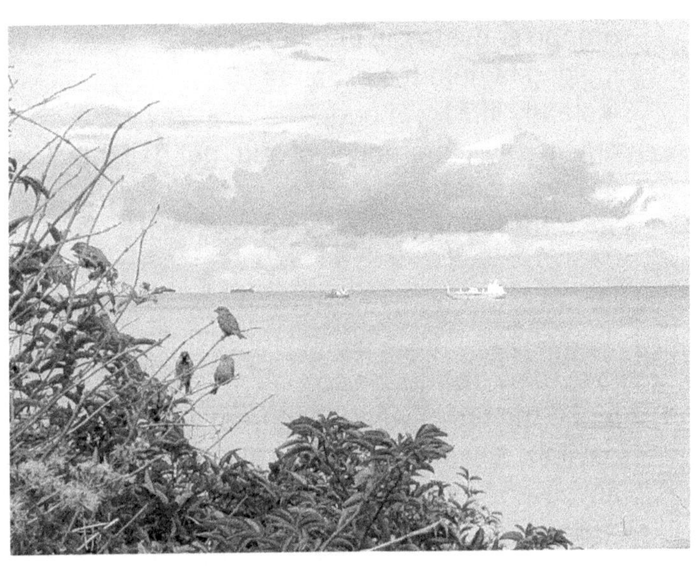

Summer Thoughts

Holding on to the last breath of summer
orange sunsets slip into my mind
looking far into the distance
instantly lifts my mood
drawn to the memories of summer delights
always there for me to recall
yesterday swings into tomorrow

Home is where my heart is
our sense within, a feeling
love to be beside the sea
ignite the fire of wandering free
daylight dawns, the sunrise glows
always

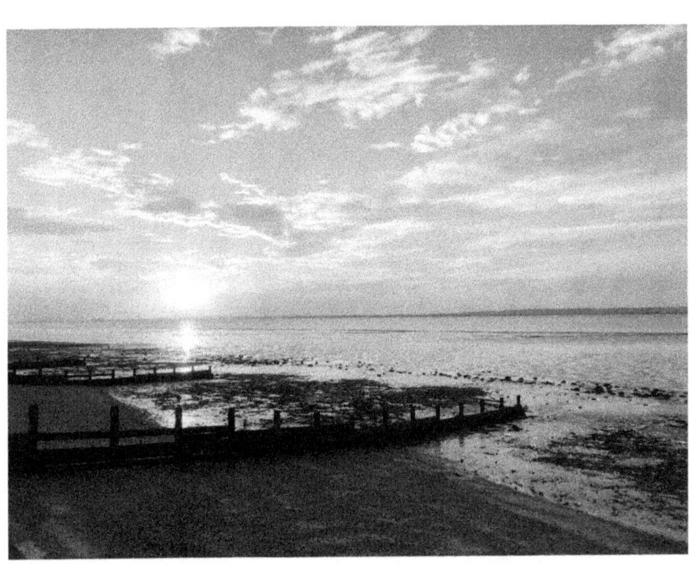

The Sea's Gift

Rising, swelling, sloshing about
ever there, forever no doubt
wondrous feeling, windswept hair
visual landscape, no compare!

Softly, sweeping, lapping away
ever there, forever a day
emotions deepen, ebbing flow
sensual feelscape, such glow!

Moonlit, twinkling, milling now
ever there, forever but how?
spirits evoked, loving touch
mystical dreamscape, so much!

Sunshine, rising, glistening delight
ever there, forever alight
soulful cleansing, giving hope
miracle seascape, I can cope!

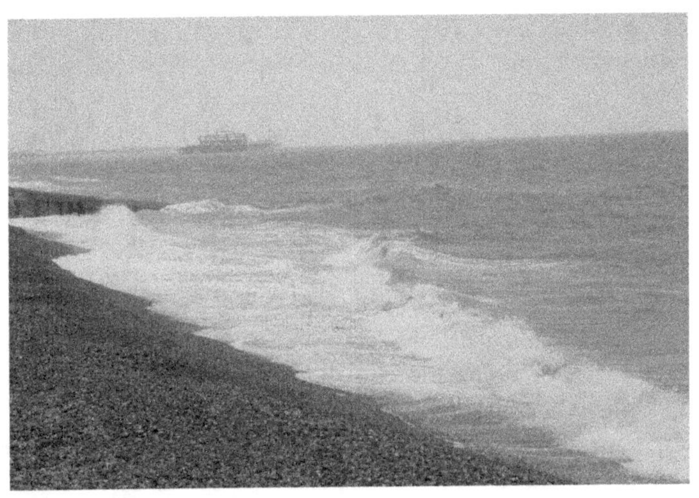

Author's endnotes

1. The clock is a sketch I made during one of the lockdowns in 2020 after an online art lesson from a friend. It is my nanny's clock and reminds me of my nanny and grandad's lovely home where I spent much time visiting in my childhood. I felt this poem, written some years back, goes well with it. Time can be elusive when we are under pressure, or elongated, perhaps when doing something creative and experiencing 'flow', something I experienced while sketching this clock as a non-artist.

2. This is Patcham Windmill near where I grew up. I took this photo on the Downs (Green Ridge, Brighton) in 2021. It looks very different from how I recall it from my childhood, especially as there is a dew pond that was created in 2000. In its place, there used to be a big dip and in the winter when it snowed heavily children used to sledge down it. The haiku was written while co-facilitating a creative workshop with the Recovery and Wellbeing College in Kent prior to the pandemic.

3. I recall writing Paradice when we had heavy snow and it was difficult to get out of the close where we lived. It was lovely going for a short walk in the freshly-fallen snow. The photo was taken at that time and I wrote the poem looking out from my second-floor townhouse bedroom window. I later carried out a visual sociology assignment on 'the street where I live', seeing such a familiar location from a different perspective.

4. I love this Furry Magical Moments photo that inspired the poem. It reminds me of a wonderful day out at the zoo in Wales. It was a very special experience walking through the Lemurs' large enclosure and it was mesmerising watching them.

5. Tenby in Wales is one of my favourite places and this poem was written after a wonderful spontaneous visit by train when I had a special spiritual experience.

6. I wrote 'I am Life' while on a train to Brighton that was held up en route. Sitting quietly in the stillness, it was a different experience taking in the railway-line environment and the poem captured the moment. The photo is one I took near where I live now, neighbouring the Peak District.

7. This photo was taken near Stone Bay in Broadstairs and not far from Viking Bay in the town centre, you can see little white sailing boats. I either wrote the poem sitting in my car or I was relaxing in one of the sister hotel lounges at Viking Bay and Botany Bay after taking the photo. I spent many a pleasant hour at both the Royal Albion Hotel and The Botany Bay Hotel taking in the seaside view and people-watching with a notebook and pen alongside my hot chocolate. If I was early enough for breakfast, I enjoyed toast with marmalade.

8. The Seaside Community poem was written on a scrap of paper when I was in the midst of creating a new Drawn by the Sea book with Scottish artist Stewart Morrison during the 2020 lockdowns. It somehow just appeared on the page in scrawling handwriting. It captured the essence of something that really helped provide me with a positive focus at such a difficult time. I chose this photo because I loved the way the little birds were gathering and singing merrily away while I was wandering around taking photos. It captured community and friendship and it is another photo I love as it takes me back to that time and place.

9. This poem was written while I was much enjoying living by the sea in Broadstairs on the Isle of Thanet in Kent. It felt such a special time for so many reasons. I had achieved a dream to live by the sea and it felt like a holiday, even though I still worked part of the time. It joins Brighton and Tenby as the places I feel the most connection to and provides that deep sense of belonging in relation to the sea. Also a member of this elite group is Allhallows in Kent, where I enjoyed many happy years with family in the caravan we had. The skyscapes at Allhallows, by the Thames Estuary, are amazing. If I caught sight of a beautiful sky as the sun was setting, I was just a short walk away from this view to grab a few shots.

10. A pebbled beach with pier in the distance, reminding me of my home town of Brighton. The poem speaks for itself and has brought me home.

Waves and Pebbles Publishing is my own publishing imprint. Other publications include:

Life Happens Live Happy (2019). Based on my own experience of being diagnosed with Acute Promyelocytic Leukaemia and aimed at anyone going through disruption in their life that is affecting their well-being.

Writing Back to Happiness. How to write the little stories in life (2022) In January 2019 I ran an eight-week "Life Story Writing" course as part of a local initiative to enrich the lives of the over 50's. Based on my own creative coaching approach and rooted in sense of belonging, through sharing our journey the book aims to inspire the reader to write and share the little stories in life - past memories, present experiences and future dreams. This book is about the friendship group that developed, the writing that arose and throughout the book there are "Life exploration activities" and lists of random story prompts and how to use them.

Books created in collaboration with Kirkcudbright-based Scottish fine artist Stewart Morrison and involving special collections of Stewart's art:

Drawn by the Sea - a collaborative art project The Isle of Thanet (2019). This book was born out of my carrying out a visual sociology assignment at Stone Bay in Broadstairs and communicating with Stewart about what I could see.

Drawn by the Sea 2020 Scottish Coastal Communities. A journey around the coast of Scotland in words and pictures. A book Stewart and I decided to create together during the lockdowns of 2020 based on a journey that Stewart was aiming to do and including places he had already visited.

Forthcoming:
Bella and Bobbles A children's story about a chocolate Labrador and a baby Seagull. A little story about dealing with change, friendship and loss inspired by a move to the Isle of Thanet coast.

To learn a little more about me, please do visit my Waves and Pebbles blog, Random thoughts and writing on life, memories and creativity, with a variable regularity of posts from 2015 onwards.

www.wavesandpebbles.blog